GRANDMA,
TELL ME

FROM:

_____

DATE:

_____

FOR YOU, BECAUSE:

_____

GRANDMA, TELL ME

A Give and Get Back Book

ELMA VAN VLIET

PARTICULAR BOOKS
an imprint of
PENGUIN BOOKS

For all the grandchildren who receive the completed book:

Enjoy reading your grandmother's stories.
I hope this becomes a true voyage of discovery.
About her, then and now, and about everything.

A NOTE FOR GRANDMA

This is your book and your story. Feel free to make it completely your own!

You can decide how much and how often you write.

Rewrite questions if you'd like to answer them differently.

Add pictures you'd like to share.

Whatever feels right to you.

When you're done, give the book back to your granddaughter or grandson.

You've just shared the stories of a lifetime with someone who loves you.

BEING A
CHILD AND
GROWING UP

ABOUT BEING A CHILD

What day were you born? Were you born at home or in the hospital? _____

_____

_____

_____

_____

What is your full name? _____

_____

Do you
know why your
parents picked
your name?

What were your nicknames? _____

_____

_____

_____

What were you like as a child?

Were you
shy or
outgoing?

What imaginary games did you play as a child?

ABOUT BEING A CHILD

How do you remember your childhood?

Are
they happy
memories?

What people or things were important to you then?

_____ What illnesses did you have as a child?

Did you ever
have to stay
in the
hospital?

_____ What were your favourite toys?

ABOUT BEING A CHILD

What games did you like? Did you play any games _____

that aren't played anymore? _____

_____

_____

_____

_____

_____

_____

_____

_____

Who was your favourite playmate? _____

_____

_____

_____

_____

_____

_____

_____

_____

_____

What did you do in the evenings and on the weekends?

What did you do during school holidays?

ABOUT BEING A CHILD

What sort of books did you read as a child?

Did your
family read
a lot?

What was your favourite day of the week?

And your favourite day of the year?

Why was
that day so
special?

What did you like most about growing up in the time you did?

space
for pictures . . .

... and more stories
and memories

space
for pictures . . .

. . . and more stories
and memories

ABOUT YOUR FAMILY

What are your parents' names? _____

_____

_____

_____

_____

Where and when were they born? _____

_____

_____

_____

_____

Where and when were your grandparents born? _____

_____

_____

_____

_____

_____

_____

Do you know how your grandparents met? _____

_____

_____

_____

_____

_____

Did you know your grandparents?

Were you
close to
them?

What were your grandfathers' jobs? Did your grandmothers work as well?

ABOUT YOUR FAMILY

What are your fondest memories of your grandparents?

_____

_____

_____

_____

_____

_____

_____

_____

_____

_____

_____

Was extended family important to you and your parents and siblings?

_____

_____

_____

Did you
see them
regularly?

_____

_____

_____

_____

Did you have favourite aunts and uncles? Who were they?

What did
you like
about them?

Who was the black sheep?

ABOUT YOUR FAMILY

What were different family members known for?

Did your family members talk about the past a lot?

What did they usually discuss?

What were your parents like as parents?

How would you describe their relationship?

Were they
old-fashioned
or more
modern?

ABOUT YOUR FAMILY

Do you know how your parents met? _____

Did they talk about that time? _____

_____

_____

_____

_____

_____

_____

_____

_____

What role did religion play in your parents' lives? _____

_____

Were you brought up religiously? _____

_____

_____

_____

What was your father's job? _____

_____

_____

_____

_____

What was your father like?

How was your relationship with him?

ABOUT YOUR FAMILY

What fond memories do you have of your father? _____

_____

_____

_____

_____

_____

_____

_____

_____

Did your mother work? If yes, what job did she have? _____

_____

_____

_____

_____

_____

_____

_____

_____

_____

What was your mother like?

How was your relationship with her?

ABOUT YOUR FAMILY

What memories of your mother do you cherish most? _____

_____

_____

_____

_____

_____

_____

_____

How did your parents spend their free time? _____

_____

_____

_____

_____

_____

_____

_____

_____

_____

_____

Are you more like your father or your mother in looks? And in personality?

How can
you tell?

What important life lessons did your parents pass on to you?

25

space
for pictures . . .

. . . and more stories
and memories

space
for pictures . . .

. . . and more stories
and memories

ABOUT YOUR PARENTS
AND SIBLINGS

How many children did your parents have? _____

What are your brothers' and sisters' names? When were they born? _____

_____

_____

_____

_____

_____

_____

_____

_____

_____

Growing up, who did you spend the most time with? _____

_____

_____

_____

Were your
personalities
alike or
were they
different?

_____

_____

_____

_____

_____

What kind of a family were you?

What was the best part about your family?

ABOUT YOUR PARENTS AND SIBLINGS

How did your father's role in raising you _____

compare to your mother's? _____

_____

_____

Were your clothes new or hand-me-downs? _____

_____

_____

_____

_____

_____

_____

As a child, how did you dress? _____

_____

_____

_____

_____

_____

_____

_____

_____

_____

_____

How did you and your siblings help around the house?

Were there certain days on which housework and chores were done?

ABOUT YOUR PARENTS
AND SIBLINGS

What technological advances changed your family's life the most?

What impact did the technology of the day have on

household needs and housework?

Do you
remember
the sounds?

What things did your family always do together?

What radio programmes, television shows or films

did your family enjoy together?

ABOUT YOUR PARENTS
AND SIBLINGS

Did your family have a television? _____

_____

_____

Which
shows did
you like?

_____

_____

_____

_____

_____

_____

Where did you live and what kind of house did you have? _____

Do you remember the address? _____

_____

_____

_____

Did your
family ever
move?

_____

_____

What was your bedroom like? Was it your own, or did you share?

What smells and sounds still remind you of the home you grew up in?

ABOUT YOUR PARENTS
AND SIBLINGS

What was your neighbourhood like?

Were you
close to the
neighbours?

Where did you buy food? And how often?

What were your favourite foods when you were a child?

And what foods did you really dislike?

What was your favourite dish? Do you know the recipe?

What did you eat at typical family dinners?

ABOUT YOUR PARENTS
AND SIBLINGS

What did your family eat on special occasions?

Do you have things in your house that have been in the family for a long time?

How did you celebrate your birthday when you were a child?

What did
you like
most about
that day?

What is the best birthday present you ever received?

ABOUT YOUR PARENTS
AND SIBLINGS

What winter holidays did your family celebrate, and how? _____

_____

_____

_____

_____

_____

_____

_____

_____

_____

_____

What did you do on New Year's Eve? _____

_____

_____

_____

Were you
allowed to
stay up until
midnight on
New Year's Eve?

_____

_____

_____

_____

What other events did you celebrate together? And how?

Did you ever go on family outings?

Where did you go and what did you do?

ABOUT YOUR PARENTS
AND SIBLINGS

As a family, how did you communicate your feelings?

Did you talk
a lot or
very little?

What hard times did you go through as a family?

What childhood memories do you look back on with a smile?

Why
these?

What do you think is the biggest difference between growing up then and now?

space
for pictures . . .

... and more stories
and memories

space
for pictures . . .

. . . and more stories
and memories

ABOUT GROWING UP
AND BECOMING AN ADULT

How old were you when you first went to school?_____

What was the name of your school?_____
_____

How did you get to school? _____
_____
_____

What did you like most about school? _____
_____
_____
_____
_____
_____
_____
_____

What did a school day look like then? What time did you start?_____
_____
_____

Did you
have certain
days or parts
of days off?
_____
_____
_____
_____
_____
_____

Can you recall a moment in which you had a great time at school?

Did you ever misbehave at school? If so, what did you do?

ABOUT GROWING UP
AND BECOMING AN ADULT

What did you call your teachers?

Did you have a favourite teacher? What was his or her name?

Why was
that teacher
special
to you?

Were there any teachers you disliked? Why?

What did you want to be when you grew up?

Were you a model student or did you dislike school?

Did you have
a favourite
subject?
What subjects
did you dislike?

What did you like to do after school?

ABOUT GROWING UP
AND BECOMING AN ADULT

What were you like as a teenager? How did you see the world?

What memories can you recall about school?

What did you do after secondary school? What path did you follow?

Were you happy with the path you chose?

ABOUT GROWING UP
AND BECOMING AN ADULT

What were the most important world events as you were growing up? _____

_____

_____

_____

_____

_____

_____

_____

_____

_____

What were your hobbies? What did you like doing? _____

_____

_____

_____

_____

_____

_____

_____

_____

_____

What music did you listen to?

Did you
have a
favourite
artist?

Where did you and your friends go out?

ABOUT GROWING UP
AND BECOMING AN ADULT

What was fashion like back then? What did you like to wear?

Did you have a job growing up? If so, what was it?

Do you remember how much you earned?

Were you living at home at the time?

ABOUT GROWING UP
AND BECOMING AN ADULT

Who were your friends?

Are you still in touch with friends from back then?

How did your relationship with your parents change as
you became more independent?

Did you feel you made your parents proud? Why or why not?

ABOUT GROWING UP
AND BECOMING AN ADULT

When did you move out of your childhood home? What was your next home like?

Which of your jobs did you enjoy the most? Why?

What do you think is the biggest difference between

studying and working then and now?

What is your best piece of advice when it comes to studying and working?

space
for pictures . . .

space
for pictures . . .

. . . and more stories
and memories

LOVE AND BECOMING A GRANDMOTHER

ABOUT LOVE

When you were young, what was dating like? _____

_____

_____

_____

_____

_____

_____

_____

_____

How did your parents feel about you dating? _____

_____

_____

_____

_____

_____

_____

_____

_____

_____

_____

Can you recall the first time you fell in love? And with whom?

Did you fall
in love easily?

Were you comfortable around boys, or were you shy?

ABOUT LOVE

Did your school offer sexual education? _____ _____

Who taught this subject and how? _____

_____

_____

_____

_____

_____

_____

Did you go on a lot of dates when you were young? _____

_____

_____

_____

_____

_____

Did you ever have your heart broken? How did you cope with that? _____

_____

_____

_____

_____

When and how did you meet my grandfather?

Was it love at first sight?

How did
you know he
liked you?

What was your first date like?

ABOUT LOVE

What did you like most about my grandfather?

Did he propose to you? How old were you and how did he do it?

Did you
need your
parents'
consent to
get married?

What was your wedding day like?

What was
the date?

Did you go on a honeymoon? Where?

ABOUT LOVE

Did you continue working after your wedding? What job did you have then? _____

_____

Did you work
full time? _____

_____

_____

_____

How long have you been or were you together? _____

_____

_____

_____

_____

_____

What is your best advice for a good relationship? _____

_____

_____

_____

_____

_____

_____

_____

What should one avoid in a relationship?

Did you always want to be a mother?

How old
were you
when you
became a
mother?

ABOUT LOVE

How did you find out you were pregnant with my mother or father?

_____

_____

_____

_____

_____

Do you
remember
how you
felt?

_____

_____

_____

What was my mother or father like as a child?

_____

_____

_____

_____

_____

_____

_____

_____

_____

Did you raise your children differently from the way your parents raised you?

What was
the biggest
difference?

What did you like most about being a mother? And what did you find challenging?

space
for pictures . . .

... and more stories
and memories

space
for pictures . . .

. . . and more stories
and memories

ABOUT BEING A GRANDMOTHER

How old were you when you first became a grandmother?

Do you remember where you were when I was born?

How did you hear
about my birth?

Did you know beforehand if I was going to be a girl or a boy?

Do you enjoy having grandchildren as much as you enjoyed having children?

What are
the biggest
differences?

Did becoming a grandmother change you? How?

ABOUT BEING A GRANDMOTHER

What is the biggest difference between your grandmothers _____

and the grandmother that you are? _____

_____

Do you
have things
in common?

_____

_____

_____

_____

_____

_____

_____

What do you enjoy most about being a grandmother? _____

_____

_____

_____

_____

_____

_____

_____

_____

_____

_____

What are your favourite moments with your grandchildren?

What is your best parenting advice?

And what
should
a parent
avoid?

space
for pictures . . .

. . . and more stories
and memories

space
for pictures . . .

. . . and more stories
and memories

ALL YOUR
FAVOURITES

ABOUT SPARE TIME, HOBBIES AND TRAVELLING

How did you like to spend your spare time when you were younger?

What were your favourite travel destinations?

Why those places?

Where did you go on your very first holiday?

Who did you
go with?

Do you have a favourite holiday memory?

ABOUT SPARE TIME, HOBBIES AND TRAVELLING

What places do you think everyone should visit?_____

_____

_____

_____

_____

_____

_____

_____

_____

_____

Has your taste in music changed over the years? What did you like to listen to _____

when you were younger and what do you like to listen to now? _____

_____

_____

_____

_____

_____

_____

_____

What are your hobbies now?

Do you play any sports? Are they the same ones you

played when you were younger?

ABOUT SPARE TIME, HOBBIES AND TRAVELLING

What makes you so excited you'd drop everything to talk about it?

What is your favourite food?

When did
you first
try it?

What is the best restaurant you have ever been to?

Where is it?

What are your three favourite books?

ABOUT SPARE TIME, HOBBIES AND TRAVELLING

What does a perfect weekend look like to you?

What are your favourite TV programmes?

What programmes do you dislike? Why?

What is the best film you've ever seen?

space
for pictures . . .

. . . and more stories
and memories

space
for pictures . . .

. . . and more stories
and memories

WHO
YOU ARE
NOW

ABOUT MEMORIES

What world events have influenced your life the most? _____

How
did they
influence it? _____

Is there a song, scent or something else that always brings back a fond memory? _____

Which of your dreams have come true?

What dreams would you still like to fulfill?

Do you have a motto or phrase you live by?

ABOUT MEMORIES

What is one of your greatest accomplishments? Was it difficult to achieve?

What goals would you still like to reach?

Have you ever met a famous person?

Who was it and what did you think of them?

What life lessons would you like to pass on to me?

Is there a joke or funny memory that still makes you laugh to this day?

ABOUT MEMORIES

Which life events made the biggest impression on you?

What time in your life makes you feel the most nostalgic?

What are the best decisions you've made in your life?

What regrets do you have, big or small?

ABOUT MEMORIES

What is the best resolution you ever made?

If you had the chance, which moments in your life would you like to live all over again?

What historic events do you feel honoured to have experienced?

Which historical figures do you admire?

Why?

ABOUT MEMORIES

Which people in your life do you owe a lot to?

Who did
you learn the
most from?

What is the greatest difference between the person you were

in the past and the person you are now?

Were there any important people in your life you had to say good-bye to?

How did
you deal
with that
loss?

space
for pictures . . .

. . . and more stories
and memories

space
for pictures . . .

. . . and more stories
and memories

ABOUT THOUGHTS, DESIRES AND DREAMS

What three things are truly important in life?

How important is your home to you?

What is your favourite place in your house?

_____Who inspires you?
_____
_____
_____
_____ Why
_____ these
_____ people?
_____
_____
_____
_____
_____
_____
_____ Which famous people do you admire? Why?
_____
_____
_____
_____
_____
_____
_____
_____
_____

ABOUT THOUGHTS,
DESIRES AND DREAMS

Which days of the year are special to you?

What do you
enjoy doing
most on
those days?

Which traditions do you love?

What does happiness mean to you?

Has this
changed over
the years?

What do you think are your best traits?

ABOUT THOUGHTS,
DESIRES AND DREAMS

What would you change about yourself if you could?

What things would you still like to learn?

What do you think are some of the benefits of growing older?

What makes you howl with laughter?

ABOUT THOUGHTS, DESIRES AND DREAMS

What things really move you?

What is your favourite day of the week? And your favourite month of the year?

If you could rule the world for one day, what would be your first decision?

In what ways has the world changed as you have grown older?

ABOUT THOUGHTS,
DESIRES AND DREAMS

What does friendship mean to you?

Who are
your best
friends and
why?

What is the greatest gift someone could give you?

Who helps you pull through when life gets tough?

What is one of the biggest compliments you have ever received?

ABOUT THOUGHTS, DESIRES AND DREAMS

Which places or countries would you still like to visit? _____

_____

_____

_____

_____

_____

_____

_____

_____

_____

Looking back, what were the greatest moments in your life? _____

_____

_____

_____

_____

_____

_____

_____

_____

_____

_____

Which great moments are still to come?

133

space
for pictures . . .

. . . and more stories
and memories

space
for pictures . . .

. . . and more stories
and memories

THE TWO OF US,
TOGETHER

TELL ME SOMETHING ABOUT ME

What family traits do you see in me? _____

_____

_____

_____

_____

_____

_____

_____

_____

_____

In what ways am I like you? How do you see yourself in me? _____

_____

_____

_____

_____

_____

_____

_____

_____

_____

_____

Which of our moments together would you pick if you

could go back and relive them?

What things would you still like to see and do with me?

TELL ME SOMETHING
ABOUT ME

What is your favourite thing about our relationship? What could make it even better?

What life lessons would you like to pass on to me?

Which of my choices makes you proud?

What do you find beautiful about me?

TELL ME SOMETHING
ABOUT ME

What have you learned from me?

What dreams do you have for me?

Is there anything you've always wanted to tell me?

Are there any questions you would like to ask me?

space
for pictures . . .

. . . and more stories
and memories

space
for pictures . . .

. . . and more·stories
and memories

space .
for pictures . . .

. . . and more stories
and memories

PARTICULAR BOOKS

UK | USA | Canada | Ireland | Australia
India | New Zealand | South Africa

Penguin Books is part of the Penguin Random House group of companies
whose addresses can be found at global.penguinrandomhouse.com.

First published in the Netherlands as *Oma, vertel eens* by Spectrum,
an imprint of Uitgeverij Unieboek, Houten 2015
First published in Great Britain by Particular Books 2019
001

Printed and bound in Italy by LEGO S.p.A.

A CIP catalogue record for this book is available from the British Library

ISBN: 978–0–241–36723–0

www.greenpenguin.co.uk

MIX
Paper from
responsible sources
FSC® C018179

Penguin Random House is committed to a
sustainable future for our business, our readers
and our planet. This book is made from Forest
Stewardship Council® certified paper.